Area 52

A Comedy Script Book

Pilot Episode

It Is Rocket Science

Written by
De-ann Black

A work fiction

Toffee Apple Publishing

Published by Toffee Apple Publishing

Area 52: A Comedy Script Book

First edition 2011

ISBN-13: 978-1-908072-37-5

Toffee Apple Publishing

INTRODUCTION

Somewhere in the heart of rural Scotland is a well–kept secret — a hidden location for a self–assembly business that manufactures traditional English, Scottish and Irish pubs ready–made and flat–packed to be sold on the international market.

Business is starting to thrive for the owner, Fergus, and the two lads who work for him — Alvie and Teapot. Orders are coming in from buyers in Europe and America. This is spectacular news for Fergus who has found a special way to create these pubs. It's astonishing what you can do with a hammer, nails, varnished newspapers, old photographs of someone's grandfather and sticky backed plastic.

But with success comes competition. How long will it be before someone else jumps on the bandwagon and manufactures Fergus' pubs for sale abroad? For this reason, Fergus protects his location and methods fiercely from prying eyes. He moves from London up to a derelict croft in the wilds of Scotland that was left to him by his late grandmother. Within the basic workshop of Area 52, Fergus and his team go to great lengths to protect their production methods.

Unfortunately, the area that Fergus unwittingly names Area 52 (sums are not his strong point), is part of a secret rocket science base where three rocket scientists (Professor Prith, Nora Blonde and Jack) work on space related projects. One lot doesn't know about the other — at least not at first.

When Fergus finds out his secret stronghold is compromised by the rocket scientists, he's determined to fight for his territory, especially when he's about to expand his pub production. The new thistle logos are already at the printers.

The sign outside his secret business reads: UFO and has an entirely different meaning than sighting flying saucers.

Sets:

Only two minimal sets needed. (No OUTDOOR shots). No OUTDOOR views are ever shown.

Although this story is situated in the wilds of Scotland, only two basic INDOOR sets are required:

THE WORKROOM — where Fergus, Alvie and Teapot work/office area and home–from–home.

Note: the MAIN WORKSHOP where they make the flat–pack pubs is never shown.

No views of what the characters see on their computer screens, or via the periscope, are shown.

THE ROCKET SCIENCE ROOM — a cross between a grocers shop and a basic scientists office where the three scientists work.

Characters:

Flat–pack pub builders:

FERGUS — Londoner, owner of the business. Rather eccentric and paranoid, but rightly so.

ALVIE — a friend from London who works for Fergus. On the run from his past, unaware that few can be bothered chasing him.

TEAPOT — a trusted colleague and friend who completes the workmen trio. The Irishman is always putting the kettle on to make a cup of tea.

V.O. character:

RAINY the remote receptionist. Heard, never seen, works for Fergus. A mystery to everyone.

WULFF — the Scottish delivery driver who picks up the finished pubs from Fergus. He is referenced in the pilot episode, but not seen or heard until further episodes.

Rocket Scientists:

NORA BLONDE — ambitious, attractive, alluring and adventurous. Not necessarily in that order.

PROFESSOR PRITH — when it comes to his attitude and style of dress, he's stuck in a 1950s time warp. He's the only one who doesn't see a problem with this.

JACK — vain, and a bit of a nerd.

SCENE 1. INT. WORKROOM — NIGHT 1 [22.00]

FERGUS AND **ALVIE** ARE WORKING LATE. BOTH MEN LOOK LIKE THEY'VE BEEN IN A SAWDUST SNOWSTORM.

FERGUS (EARLY 30s, WEARING WELL–WORN JEANS AND JUMPER, HAS PROTECTIVE EYE GOGGLES PERCHED ON HIS HEAD). HE IS VARNISHING OLD NEWSPAPER CUTTINGS, WHILE **ALVIE** (LATE 20s, WEARING SIMILAR) IS STICKING A BIG LABEL ON TO A LONG, FLAT CARDBOARD PACKING BOX. THE LABEL READS: *FERGUS' PACK–A–PUBS. TRADITIONAL FLAT–PACKED PUBS MADE BY CRAFTSMEN JOINERS.*

THE WORKROOM LOOKS LIKE A BIG GARDEN SHED. IT IS AN ORGANISED MESS — AN ODD MIX OF BASIC LABOUR TOOLS AND HI–TECH GADGETS. THIS INCLUDES SECURITY CAMERAS AND A PERISCOPE TO SPY ON ANYONE APPROACHING THE BUSINESS. THERE ARE NO WINDOWS.

A GLASS PARTITION ENCLOSES AN OFFICE SPACE (DESK, TWO COMPUTERS, OTHER COMMUNICATIONS/SECURITY GADGETS) — AND A TEA/SNACK MAKING AREA WITH MICROWAVE OVEN, THREE TEAPOTS (TWO WITH TEA COSIES), AND A SURPRISED–LOOKING STUFFED CAT.

A DOOR LEADS TO THE MAIN WORKSHOP (MAIN WORKSHOP IS NEVER SEEN). THE WORKROOM ALSO HAS A FRONT DOOR ENTRANCE.

FERGUS:
You have to ask yourself — why was he walking into a dinosaur museum looking for chicken nuggets?

ALVIE:
The thing that bothers me is — why was Teapot looking for chicken when we sent him for pizza?

FERGUS:
And when did they build a dinosaur museum in the town? Where did they get the dinosaurs?

TEAPOT (LATE 20s, WEARING SAME WORKWEAR AS **FERGUS** AND **ALVIE**), COMES RUNNING INTO THE WORKROOM FROM OUTSIDE.

TEAPOT:
(SHOUTS) I've just seen a gorgeous blonde wearing a silver swimsuit diving into the loch.

FERGUS:
Have you been eating gumdrops again?

TEAPOT:
(HESITATES)

FERGUS:
(ACCUSINGLY) Green ones?

TEAPOT:
Eh, no, maybe, but that's got nothing to do with it. I saw her. She was all lit up in the moonlight.

ALVIE:
Just like last week when you saw an alien spaceship hovering over the outside loo?

TEAPOT:
Fine, suit yourselves. I'm going to get the nightsights. I want a good look at her.

TEAPOT OPENS A CUPBOARD FULL OF ODDITIES AND GADGETS. HE SNATCHES THE NIGHTSIGHT BINOCULARS AND HURRIES OUTSIDE.

FERGUS:
(TO ALVIE) What do you think?

ALVIE:
Oh yes, there's going to be a gorgeous blonde swimming in the wilds of Scotland, in the middle of October, at this time of night.

CURIOSITY GETS THE BETTER OF **FERGUS.** HE PUTS DOWN HIS GLUE BRUSH AND PEERS THROUGH THE PERISCOPE TO SPY ON **TEAPOT. ALVIE** JOINS HIM.

ALVIE:
Can you see her?

FERGUS:
It's too dark. I can't see a thing . . . wait a minute, there's Teapot. He's running like blazes towards the loch.

ALVIE:
Give us a look.

FERGUS:
(HOGS THE PERISCOPE) Use the security cameras, switch to infrared.

ALVIE HURRIES OVER TO ONE OF THE OFFICE COMPUTERS AND SCANS THE AREA OUTSIDE.

ALVIE:
Not that I believe him for a minute. I mean, there's nobody for miles, never mind a blonde in a silver swimsuit. Unless of course . . .

FERGUS:
What?

ALVIE:
Nothing.

FERGUS:
Unless she's a spy, sent to snoop on our plans.

ALVIE:
Nah. Who'd go to all that bother just to steal your secrets? You're getting paranoid again.

FERGUS:
What's the definition of paranoid?

ALVIE:
Having delusions of being watched, hounded and spied on.

FERGUS:
So that makes me right, not paranoid. There are sharks out there with plenty of money to throw around. If they found out my techniques, how we build our flat–pack pubs, they'd steal the idea and make a fortune for themselves.

ALVIE PEERS AT THE COMPUTER SCREEN, SEARCHING FOR THE BLONDE.

FERGUS:
(PEERING THROUGH PERISCOPE) There's no one out there. The only thing I can see is that idiot, Teapot.

ALVIE:
(HAS A FINAL CHECK ON SECURITY CAMERA) Definitely no blondes swimming in the loch.

FERGUS CLOSES THE PERISCOPE. **ALVIE** STOPS SEARCHING THE SECURITY SYSTEM. THEY GO BACK TO WORK. **FERGUS** VARNISHES THE LAST FEW PIECES OF OLD NEWSPAPER. **ALVIE** STICKS A LABEL ON THE CARDBOARD BOX.

FERGUS:
Two years, that's all we need. The business is picking up fast. We've had double the orders since last month. But that's where the danger lies. With success comes competition.

ALVIE:
The competition's never going to find you here. It's barely on the map. Bleak, remote — even satellite can't see us. We've got it all to ourselves. It's brilliant, like living on the far side of the moon.

FERGUS:
Only more private. These space nerds nowadays have telescopes powerful enough to spot an earwig's eyebrow on Mars. It's a shame their satellites can't see a thing through the grey mist and rain. Just miles of nothing.

ALVIE:
Nobody but the three of us.

TEAPOT COMES RUNNING INTO THE WORKSHOP CARRYING THE NIGHTSIGHT BINOCULARS.

TEAPOT:
(EXCITED) Her name's Nora – and she's fantastic.

FERGUS:
You met her? You actually spoke to her?

TEAPOT:
No, no . . . she was on the other side of the loch.

ALVIE:
So how do you know her name's Nora?

TEAPOT:
It was printed on her swimsuit. N.O.R.A.

FERGUS:
Are you having us on?

TEAPOT:
Didn't you see her ripples in the moonlight? I thought you'd be spying through the periscope and the infrared.

FERGUS:
We had a look, but all we could see was you running around with a pair of nightsights glued to your eyeballs.

TEAPOT:
Nora was on the far side of the loch. I saw her shimmering silver figure emerge from the water in the moonlight and then . . . she disappeared into the night . . .

FERGUS:
In your dreams.

TEAPOT:
(REFERS TO HIS HI–TECH WRISTWATCH) I've got some snaps of her.

ALVIE:
When did you get that?

TEAPOT:
Last week. It can take photos, play music, send e–mails and calculates the exact time everywhere in the world from the Outer Hebrides to Honolulu.

FERGUS:
When are you ever going to need the exact time in Honolulu?

SFX: A BING–BONG CHIME INTERRUPTS. A MESSAGE IS RELAYED OVER THEIR REMOTE INTERCOM SYSTEM. AN ATTRACTIVE

SOUNDING WOMAN'S VOICE IS HEARD VIA SPEAKERS IN THE WORKROOM.

RAINY: (V.O.)
This is Rainy your remote receptionist. Are you there boys? One of your bleepers is still active. Are you working late again?

FERGUS:
(VERY POLITE) Yes, just putting the finishing touches to a last minute order.

ALVIE MIMICS FERGUS. **FERGUS** GLARES AT HIM.

ALVIE:
(WHISPERS TO TEAPOT) He's got a crush on Rainy the remote receptionist.

FERGUS:
(TO ALVIE) Get lost.

<u>ALVIE:</u>
You talk funny when you speak to her.

<u>FERGUS:</u>
I do not.

<u>ALVIE:</u>
Yes you do, your voice goes all hoity–toity.

<u>RAINY:</u> (V.O.)
I have something for you, Fergus. Would you like me to give it to you?

<u>ALVIE:</u>
(IMITATES FERGUS) Yes, please.

<u>RAINY:</u> (V.O.)
It's an urgent message. I'm sending it to your secure e–mail Inbox . . . now.

SFX: PING. THE E–MAIL ARRIVES.

FERGUS:
(CHECKS COMPUTER) Got it, thanks.

RAINY: (V.O.)
I, eh . . . I don't usually get personal with my clients, but I was wondering, Fergus . . . your voice has an intriguing wobble in it. Did you used to be a sailor?

FERGUS:
Yes, Royal Navy, five years. I was a mid–shipman joiner–electrician and an expert in semaphore. I've even taught the lads here how to signal with their flags in a force 10 gale. Not many men could withstand their pennants being exposed to that sort of weather.

RAINY: (V.O.)
Hello sailor. Ahem, but back to business. As you'll see from the e–mail, it's a message from a potential customer in Honolulu about your new Scottish themed pack–a–pubs. He likes the curve of your lucky horseshoe bar, but he wants a glimpse of your thistle before he goes ahead with the order. And he's asked me to arrange a remote meeting — a web conference with you tomorrow afternoon at 2pm — Honolulu time.

FERGUS AND **ALVIE** LOOK AT **TEAPOT**. HE SLAPS HIS HAND FIRMLY OVER HIS WRISTWATCH TO PREVENT THEM FROM SEEING THE TIME. A CHASE, A HARMLESS WRESTLE AND A KERFUFFLE FOLLOWS. **ALVIE** EMERGES TRIUMPHANT HOLDING **TEAPOT'S** WATCH. **FERGUS** GRABS THE WATCH AND FIDDLES WITH THE BUTTONS. THE DEVICE MAKES VARIOUS BEEPING SOUNDS. **FERGUS** FINDS THE CORRECT TIME.

<u>FERGUS:</u>
(TO RAINY) That'll be one o'clock in the morning here.

<u>RAINY:</u> (V.O.)
(IMPRESSED) You really are well travelled.

TEAPOT GOES TO SPEAK UP AND COMPLAIN, BUT **FERGUS** GETS HIM IN A HEADLOCK AND PREVENTS HIM FROM SPEAKING.

SCENE 2. INT. WORKROOM — NEXT DAY [17.00]

FERGUS, **ALVIE** AND **TEAPOT** ARE WORKING HARD. ALL OF THEM LOOK LIKE THEY'VE BEEN IN A SAWDUST SNOWSTORM. **ALVIE** AND **TEAPOT** ARE CUTTING OUT THE LAST PIECES OF A LARGE CARDBOARD THISTLE LOGO, WHILE **FERGUS** POLISHES AN OLD BANJO.

TEAPOT:
Phew! The last one. Three complete pubs today. Must be a record.

FERGUS GIVES A TRIUMPHANT STRUM ON THE BANJO, AND THEN PACKS IT INTO A CARDBOARD BOX.

FERGUS:
Wulff's going to pick the order up at midnight. So after this, we'll get our tea and take a break.

ALVIE:
Does Wulff know the secret code?

FERGUS:
Two flashes and a triple beep.

TEAPOT:
I'm going to keep a lookout for Nora tonight.

FERGUS:
You're winding us up again.

TEAPOT:
(SHAKES HIS HEAD) I definitely saw her, but when you fiddled with my watch you deleted all the pictures I had. I tried to download them on to the computer but they're gone.

ALVIE:
(TO TEAPOT) Yeah, right.

SFX: A RED LIGHT FLASHES ON THE WALL. **FERGUS** HURRIES OVER TO THE PERISCOPE. **ALVIE** HURRIES TO THE COMPUTER TO CHECK THE SECURITY ALARM SYSTEM.

FERGUS:
Vehicle approaching the outer perimeter.

TEAPOT:
Who is it?

FERGUS:
Just waiting for the fog to clear a bit. It's a van.

TEAPOT:
Wulff's delivery van?

FERGUS:
Nope.

ALVIE:
There's something odd sticking out the top of the roof. It looks like . . .

SFX: ICE CREAM VAN MUSIC CAN BE HEARD. **TEAPOT** LEANS OVER AND LOOKS AT THE COMPUTER SCREEN.

TEAPOT:
An ice cream van. What I wouldn't give for a raspberry wafer and a packet of crisps. My throat feels like the inside of a weasel's burrow.

ALVIE:
(SIGHS AND LOOKS WISTFULLY AT THE COMPUTER SCREEN) Tempting, isn't it?

FERGUS:
(NODS) Could be a trick to entice us out. First a blonde, then a double nougat.

TEAPOT:
Don't be daft. It's the local ice cream van. I've seen it in the town. I'd recognise that raspberry cone anywhere.

FERGUS:
Right, I've got a plan. Teapot, strip down to your boxers.

TEAPOT HESITATES.

FERGUS:
Do you want an ice cream or not?

TEAPOT NODS RELUCTANTLY.

FERGUS:
Well, come on, hurry up. And keep your boots on.

TEAPOT:
(QUICKLY TAKES HIS TOP AND JEANS OFF)
What's the plan?

FERGUS:
Alvie, give us a couple of sticky labels with matching numbers on them.

ALVIE GRABS A COUPLE OF LABELS. **FERGUS** STICKS ONE LABEL ON **TEAPOT'S** CHEST AND ONE ON HIS BACK.

ALVIE:
Ah, a scraggy–looking hill runner with clumpy boots.

FERGUS:
Exactly. (TO TEAPOT) Pretend you were in a race and got lost in the fog. If the ice cream man asks you any awkward questions, just smile and feign being out of puff.

TEAPOT:
By the time I catch up with the van I won't need to pretend — I'll be knackered.

FERGUS:
All the more authentic. Now hurry up.

TEAPOT:
How come it's me that has to go? It's freezing fog out there.

ALVIE:
Because you've got the leanest physique, I'm a rotten liar, and Fergus always looks shifty.

FERGUS GIVES **TEAPOT** A TEN POUND NOTE FROM HIS TROUSER POCKET.

TEAPOT:
(FLICKS A BUTTON ON HIS WATCH) Okay – what do you want?

TEAPOT HOLDS UP HIS WATCH WHILE **FERGUS** AND **ALVIE** SPEAK THEIR ORDERS INTO IT.

ALVIE:
(INTO WATCH) A vanilla cone and a raspberry wafer.

FERGUS:
(INTO WATCH) Double nougat with chocolate sprinkles and a packet of salt and vinegar crisps. And remember to take a different route back so they don't know whether you're coming or going.

TEAPOT NODS, ADJUSTS HIS BAGGY BOXER SHORTS AND RUNS OUTSIDE. THROUGH THE PERISCOPE AND THE SECURITY CAMERA IMAGES ON THE COMPUTER SCREEN, **FERGUS** AND **ALVIE** WATCH **TEAPOT** CHASING THE VAN.

ALVIE:
(CHEERS) Go Teapot!

FERGUS:
He could pass for a hill runner with those legs, especially in the fog.

ALVIE:

Look, he's gaining on the van. Oops, the slipstream's whipped his labels off.

FERGUS:

The ice cream man's spotted him. He's pulling over.

ALVIE:

Do you think it'll look suspicious that he's got the orders recorded in his watch?

FERGUS:

Nah, it'll be all right. Teapot's like you, he looks a right geek.

ALVIE ADJUSTS THE SECURITY SYSTEM TO GET A BETTER VIEW ON THE COMPUTER SCREEN.

ALVIE:

I can see your double nougat. Oh and there's my raspberry wafer.

FERGUS:
I'll flick the kettle on. He'll need a cup of tea to warm him up when he gets back.

ALVIE:
But we're having ice cream.

FERGUS:
You can't enjoy a wafer when you're frozen.

FERGUS GOES TO SWITCH THE KETTLE ON AND SETS UP THE CUPS FOR TEA.

ALVIE:
That's the van driving away. And Teapot's taking another route back.

SFX: A PING SOUNDS FROM **ALVIE'S** COMPUTER. HE PEERS AT THE SCREEN, AND THEN LOOKS ASTOUNDED.

FERGUS:
What is it?

ALVIE:
The pictures Teapot took of Nora. You hadn't deleted them — they've finally downloaded.

FERGUS DASHES OVER FOR A LOOK AT THE WOMAN.

FERGUS:
(ASTOUNDED) Wow!

ALVIE:
(IMPRESSED) Wow, right enough.

ALVIE SUDDENLY LOOKS PUZZLED AND FOCUSES ON HER PICTURES ON THE SCREEN.

ALVIE:
Would you look at that.

FERGUS:
What?

ALVIE:
The name on her swimsuit.

FERGUS:
Nora?

ALVIE:
Look closer, look at her dots.

FERGUS HAS A CLOSER LOOK.

FERGUS:
Oh, I see what you mean. N.O.R.A. A funny way to spell her name.

ALVIE:
What if it's not her name?

FERGUS:
(SUDDENLY SUSPICIOUS) Check it out on the Internet. See what comes up for N.O.R.A.

ALVIE TYPES THIS INTO THE COMPUTER.

ALVIE:
I've got a weird feeling about this.

FERGUS:
(NODS)

SFX: PING.

ALVIE:
(READS FROM THE SCREEN) N.O.R.A. – she belongs to some sort of space organisation. She's a rocket scientist!

FERGUS LEANS CLOSER TO READ THE INFORMATION.

FERGUS:
(READS FROM THE SCREEN) Rocket scientists located throughout the world in remote areas where they research and study scientific space phenomenon.

ALVIE:
On our doorstep.

FERGUS:
They can't be. They weren't here when we arrived last month.

ALVIE:
It all makes sense now. The silver swimsuit, the strange lights hovering over the outside loo.

FERGUS:
The constant feeling of being watched.

ALVIE:
But they're rocket scientists. They won't be interested in stealing your flat–pack pub ideas.

FERGUS:
You can never be too careful. They could talk about us in the wrong circles.

ALVIE SUDDENLY REALISES HE'S FORGOTTEN TO KEEP AN EYE ON **TEAPOT**.

ALVIE:
(SEARCHES THE SECURITY SYSTEM) Where's Teapot gone?

FERGUS HURRIES OVER TO THE PERISCOPE.

FERGUS:
I can't see him. Maybe he got lost in the fog.

ALVIE:
Spotted him. (ASTOUNDED) He's near the far side of the loch and . . . I don't believe it . . .

ALVIE AND **FERGUS** GASP AS THEY VIEW **TEAPOT** THROUGH THE PERISCOPE AND SECURITY SYSTEM.

SCENE 3. INT. ROCKET SCIENCE ROOM. SAME TIME.

PROFESSOR PRITH (50s, WEARING A WHITE COAT) IS WATCHING **TEAPOT** ON A SECURITY MONITOR. BESIDE HIM IS CATHERINE BLONDE (SHE WILL BE REFERRED TO AS **NORA BLONDE**). (**NORA** IS AGED LATE 20s, BLONDE, VERY ATTRACTIVE, CASUALLY DRESSED BUT LOOKS GLAMOROUS). **JACK** (EARLY 30s, QUITE GOOD LOOKING IN A NERDY SORT OF WAY) IS OPERATING THE SECURITY SYSTEM.

PRITH:
Whoever he is, he's not wearing any clothes.

NORA:
(LOOKS CLOSER) Really?

PRITH:
Luckily the low–lying fog is blurring his predicament.

JACK:
(TO NORA) Don't look. He's bare chested and has a wild looking hairstyle.

NORA:
The locals don't usually venture out this far. What's he up to?

PRITH:
He appears to be sending us semaphore signals using a pair of underpants and a packet of salt and vinegar crisps.

NORA:
Signal back. Ask him who he is. He could be a lurker.

PRITH SEARCHES AROUND FOR MAKESHIFT FLAGS. HE USES TWO PIECES OF SILVER CLOTH. **PRITH** THEN STANDS AT THE ENTRANCE (WE DO NOT SEE OUTSIDE). WE ONLY SEE **PRITH** SIGNALLING WITH THE FLAGS WHILE **NORA** AND **JACK** ARE BEHIND HIM IN THE ROOM.

PRITH:
(STARTS SIGNALLING) I'm a bit rusty.

NORA:
But is your semaphore any good?

PRITH:
I only remember the basics. (HE SPEAKS THE MESSAGE WHILE HE SIGNALS). Who goes there?

SCENE 4. INT. WORKROOM. SAME TIME.

FERGUS AND **ALVIE** ARE WATCHING **TEAPOT** SIGNALLING.

FERGUS:
He's definitely lost. He's asking for directions.

ALVIE:
I'd better go and get him.

FERGUS:
Hang on, someone's signalling back to him.

ALVIE:
Where?

FERGUS:
Over there, look. The guy in the white coat. His semaphore is a bit rusty.

ALVIE:

(READS THE SIGNAL) Are you bare? Stupid question. Of course he's bare, he's waving his underpants in the air.

FERGUS:

Teapot's signalling back.

SCENE 5. INT. ROCKET SCIENCE ROOM. SAME TIME.

PRITH TRIES TO DECIPHER **TEAPOT'S** NEXT MESSAGE.

PRITH:
Are you . . . I'm not sure what he's asking. Are you . . . A . . . l, Al something. Wait I've got it. Are you alive?

JACK:
(SNOOTILY) Are we alive?
NORA:
Tell him yes.

PRITH:
(SIGNALS) Yes.

SCENE 6. INT. WORKROOM. SAME TIME.

FERGUS:
(READS **TEAPOT'S** SIGNAL) Are you Alvie?

ALVIE:
Oh no, he thinks it's me.

THEY READ THE MAN IN THE WHITE COAT'S REPLY.

FERGUS:
He's said, yes.
ALVIE:
(RAGING) Liar! I'm going out to get Teapot myself.

FERGUS:
No, hang on a minute. They're only rocket scientists. We can outsmart them.

FERGUS AND **ALVIE** NOD IN AGREEMENT, AND HURRY OVER TO A BIG CUPBOARD.

SCENE 7. INT. ROCKET SCIENCE ROOM. SAME TIME.

PRITH:

The man appears to be putting his underpants back on and is heading in our direction.

JACK:

Discourage him. We don't know what he's up to. He'll compromise our security.

NORA:

What's he carrying? (PEERS AT SECURITY MONITOR) It looks like a cardboard tray with a double nougat on it.

JACK:

Bribing us with ice cream won't work.

SCENE 8. INT. WORKROOM. SAME TIME.

FERGUS AND **ALVIE** STEP OUT OF THE WALK–IN CUPBOARD. **FERGUS** IS DRESSED AS SHERLOCK HOLMES AND **ALVIE** IS WEARING A POLICEMAN'S UNIFORM AND HELMET FROM THE 1950s.

FERGUS:
I thought you said the police disguises were okay. Look at these. They're ridiculous.

ALVIE:
It's all I could get in the fancy dress shop. Proper disguises are on order, but they won't be here until next week. I thought these would be better than nothing.

FERGUS:
(SIGHS) They'll have to do. The fog will make us a bit blurry anyway, especially if we're quick.

ALVIE TIGHTENS HIS HELMET. **FERGUS** SHOWS THAT HE'S GOT AN EMERGENCY

SILVER BLANKET IN HIS CAPE POCKET FOR **TEAPOT**.

FERGUS:
We'll wrap this round Teapot. He'll be freezing.

ALVIE:
Do you think our ice cream will have melted?

FERGUS:
(GLARES) Come on, let's intercept him before the rocket scientists do.

FERGUS AND **ALVIE** HURRY OUT OF THE WORKROOM.

SCENE 9. INT. ROCKET SCIENCE ROOM. SAME TIME.

JACK:
(STUDYING THE SECURITY MONITOR) Is that Sherlock Holmes emerging from the fog?

PRITH:
(SHUDDERS) I used to have nightmares about the hounds of the Baskervilles.

NORA:
It'll be the local police. They're still rather old fashioned around here.

JACK:
Good, they've arrested that idiot and his double nougat.

PRITH:
They're wrapping him in tin foil. Is that normal?

NORA AND **JACK** SHRUG THEIR SHOULDERS.

NORA:
Now they're running off with him . . . and they've disappeared back into the fog . . .

SCENE 10. INT. WORKROOM. LATER SAME NIGHT.

FERGUS, **ALVIE** AND **TEAPOT** ARE WEARING THEIR ORDINARY WORK CLOTHES AGAIN. THE REMAINS OF THE ICE CREAM AND CRISPS FEAST LIES ON THE TABLE. THEY ARE DRINKING CUPS OF TEA.

ALVIE:
Are we scuppered?

FERGUS:
No, I'm not letting a bunch of rocket scientists ruin my business.

TEAPOT:
Have you got a plan?

FERGUS:
I've always got a plan… (GLANCES AT THE COMPUTERS).

TEAPOT:
I'll put the kettle on again.

FERGUS:
(TO ALVIE) Hope you haven't lost your touch.

ALVIE:
Never have, never will.

FERGUS AND **ALVIE** SIT IN FRONT OF THE WORKROOM'S TWO COMPUTERS.

FERGUS:
Let's see what they're up to.

FERGUS AND **ALVIE** BEGIN TO TYPE EAGERLY INTO THE COMPUTER KEYBOARDS.

TEAPOT:
Will I break open a packet of custard creams?

FERGUS:
Oh yes, it's going to be a long night.

TEAPOT:
(TO FERGUS) Are you hacking into their computer system?

FERGUS:
Nope, Alvie is.

ALVIE IS BUSY WORKING ON THIS. HE SMILES AT **TEAPOT. FERGUS** CONCENTRATES ON HIS OWN COMPUTER, ACCESSING DATA.

FERGUS:
I installed hidden cameras and other devices around the perimeter of the loch. (HE POINTS TO HIS COMPUTER SCREEN) See the wood pigeon perched in that tree over there?

TEAPOT:
(NODS) The one with the glazed look in its eyes?

FERGUS:
Yes, I made him out of bits of wood and an unravelled tea cosy.

TEAPOT LOOKS AT THE MISSING TEA COSY FROM ONE OF THE TEAPOTS.

TEAPOT:
I wondered what had happened to that.

FERGUS:
I stuck camera lenses in his eyeballs and stuffed a long–range microphone up his tail feathers.

TEAPOT:
Good job you're paranoid, eh Fergus?

FERGUS:
(GRINS)

SCENE 11. INT. ROCKET SCIENCE ROOM. SAME TIME THAT NIGHT.

THE ROCKET SCIENTISTS ARE MONITORING THEIR SECURITY SYSTEM.

PRITH:

(AGGITATED) I contacted headquarters about a possible breach of our secure location. I explained about the naked underpants waver, Sherlock Holmes and the policeman.

NORA:

What do they advise we do?

PRITH:

After ridiculing me, accusing me of being drunk, delusional or just plain loopy, they said we'll have to get on with it. So stuff 'em!

JACK:
Did you ask them to double check those old croft buildings on the far side of the loch? I'm sure I've seen strange figures coming and going at odd hours, especially when it's dark.

PRITH:
Oh, they poo–pooed that as well. Said it used to belong to an old lady, but she left it to her useless nephew, some sailor fellow down in London. But he's never bothered with it and is likely to just let it rot.

NORA:
But they all ran off in the opposite direction, *away* from the croft buildings.

PRITH:
It could have been a ruse to fool us.

JACK:
They didn't look smart enough to fool us, Prith. Anyone who semaphores with a packet of salt and vinegar crisps probably has the intelligence of a gnat.

NORA:
He could be a genius. Some men are so smart you could almost mistake them for being stupid. Look at Prith, he's a prime example.

PRITH SMILES AT THE COMPLIMENT.

JACK:
(MIFFED) Don't I look stupid enough to be clever?

NORA:
In the right light, yes. And speaking of light, it's still a full moon. I'm going to test the fabric again in the loch. See if it'll disintegrate if I expose it to cold pressure.

JACK:
I'll keep an eye on you on the monitors.

PRITH:
(INTERVENES) You'll need to test the umbrella tonight, Jack.

JACK:
(SIGHS) Oh all right.

JACK TAKES A BIG SILVER UMBRELLA OUT OF A CUPBOARD, GRABS A WARM JACKET AND STOMPS OUTSIDE.

SCENE 12. INT. WORKROOM. SAME TIME.

FERGUS SEES **JACK** ON THE SECURITY SYSTEM. **ALVIE** IS BUSY HACKING INTO THE SCIENTISTS' COMPUTER SYSTEM.

FERGUS:
That has to be one of them. He looks like a rocket scientist with that big silver umbrella.

TEAPOT:
That's not an umbrella. I've seen gadgets like that before. When I bought my watch they had all sorts of weird stuff for spying and surveillance.

FERGUS:
Is he spying on us?

TEAPOT:
He's certainly acting suspicious. What's the sound range on the wood pigeon?

FERGUS:
A hundred metres before it becomes a mumble.

TEAPOT:
Can you get the pigeon to home in on him?

FERGUS ADJUSTS THE DIRECTION OF THE PIGEON USING THE SECURITY SYSTEM ON HIS COMPUTER.

SFX: LOUD CRACKLING WITH LOTS OF HISSING INTERFERENCE.

FERGUS:
Sorry, it's the wind whistling through his tail feathers.

TEAPOT:
Turn his backside north a bit more.

FERGUS MAKES THE ADJUSTMENT AND THE SOUND BECOMES CLEARER.

ALVIE:
(SHOUTS) Bingo! We're in.

FERGUS LETS **TEAPOT** DECIPHER THE UMBRELLA SOUNDS, WHILE HE FINDS OUT WHAT THE SCIENTISTS ARE UP TO VIA **ALVIE'S** COMPUTER.

FERGUS:
What are they doing?

ALVIE:
(LAUGHS) One of them is watching over this way. There's only three of them.

FERGUS:
A level playing field then, eh?

ALVIE:
There's Professor Prith, Jack and —

TEAPOT:
(SHOUTS) Nora! She's out in the moonlight in her silver swimsuit again — and some of it's disappearing.

FERGUS AND **ALVIE** STOP WHAT THEY'RE DOING AND TAKE A LOOK. UNFORTUNATELY, **JACK** AND HIS BIG UMBRELLA GET IN THE WAY.

ALVIE:
(SHOUTS) Get out the way.

TEAPOT:
Grrrrr.

FERGUS:
Quick, let me in. (HE MOVES **TEAPOT** ASIDE AND TYPES HURRIEDLY INTO THE COMPUTER) I've got a ferret hidden in the bushes. If I can activate his eyeballs we should be able to see . . .

TEAPOT:
Nah, too late, she's wrapped herself in a parka.

SFX: CRACKLING SOUNDS COMING FROM **JACK'S** UMBRELLA.

ALVIE:
Isn't that one of those beacon transmitters that sends signals into space?

FERGUS:
Who would they be signalling to?

ALVIE:
I'll see if I can find out.

ALVIE GOES BACK TO HACKING INTO THE SCIENTISTS INFORMATION. TEAPOT READS IT TOO.

TEAPOT:
Seems like they eat, sleep and work in their secret science hideout.

ALVIE:
(NODS) It's kitted out like a cross between a space office and a mini grocers.

SCENE 13. INT. ROCKET SCIENCE ROOM. SAME TIME.

NORA:
(STILL WEARING HER PARKA) (TO PRITH) Do you think they'll pick up Jack's signal and come back tonight?

PRITH:
Sherlock Holmes and the nougat nugget?

NORA:
No – *them.*

PRITH:
Oh, *them* . . . well I've got the video cameras set up just in case. It could make us infamous if we get some clear footage of them.

NORA:
I recalibrated the spokes on Jack's umbrella, and increased the signal's wavelength by a googolplex.

PRITH:
We'd better get our goggles on then, eh?

PRITH AND **NORA** PUT ON SPACE–AGE STYLE GOGGLES. **NORA** GOES TO THE DOOR ENTRANCE AND LOOKS OUT, WHILE **PRITH** WATCHES THE MONITORS.

NORA:
Are my goggles deceiving me, or is that a monster truck reversing like mad towards Jack?

PRITH:
(INTO LOUD–SPEAKER MICROPHONE) Run Jack, run!

SCENE 14. INT. WORKROOM. SAME TIME.

SFX: TRIPLE BEEP OF A LOUD HORN.

FERGUS:
(PEERS THROUGH PERISCOPE) Two flashes and a triple beep. That'll be Wulff. I told him to reverse drive round the back to load the pubs on to the truck. I'll go and give him a hand. You two keep an eye on that idiot with the umbrella.

FERGUS GOES OUT OF THE ROOM.

TEAPOT:
Did you hear someone shouting, run Jack, run?

ALVIE:
No, couldn't hear anything for Wulff's horn. (OBSERVES JACK ON SCREEN) Mind you, the umbrella man is racing round the loch like a maniac.

TEAPOT:

The entrance to their rocket science lab must be hidden by that big tree. A right sneaky lot. What do you think Fergus will do?

ALVIE:

Stay and fight for his territory. But I reckon the rocket scientists have got as much to lose as us if people knew they were here. We've both got our secrets to hide.

TEAPOT:

I don't think they know who we are. I mean, who's ever going to suspect that we make pubs in the middle of nowhere?

SFX: TWO LOUD BEEPS OF A HORN.

ALVIE:

That's Wulff away with the pubs. Doesn't hang around, does he?

TEAPOT:

(LOOKS AT COMPUTER SCREEN) Who's that skulking near the outside loo?

ALVIE:

It's just Fergus going to the bog.

SUDDENLY A LIGHT STARTS TO DAZZLE THEM FROM THE COMPUTER SCREEN. **ALVIE** AND **TEAPOT** SHIELD
THEIR EYES.

TEAPOT QUICKLY GRABS TWO PAIRS OF RED–GLASS PROTECTIVE GOGGLES FROM A SHELF.

ALVIE:

(SHIELDS HIS EYES WITH HIS HANDS) I can't see a thing for the glare.

TEAPOT:

Here, stick these on.

ALVIE AND **TEAPOT** PUT ON THE RED GOGGLES AND THIS ALLOWS THEM TO VIEW THE SCENE.

ALVIE:
(STUNNED) Is that a . . .?

TEAPOT:
I told you there was an alien spaceship hovering over the loo last week, but you wouldn't believe me.

ALVIE:
(SUDDENLY BECOMES SUSPICIOUS) I think it's a trick of the light. I'll bet it's those sneaky scientists trying to scare us off. Underneath all that dazzle it'll be a remote control plastic model.

TEAPOT:
I never thought of that . . .

ALVIE:
We need to warn Fergus so he doesn't get frightened off.

TEAPOT ACTIVATES THE COMPUTER **FERGUS** USED TO CONTROL THE WOOD PIGEON AND THE FERRET.

TEAPOT:
I'm taking a long shot here, but did you ever notice that creepy–looking squirrel that was always hanging around the loo?

ALVIE:
The one with the glazed look in its eyes?

TEAPOT:
(SMILES) With any luck it'll have a hidden microphone up its . . . yes . . . here we are.

<u>ALVIE:</u>
(SPEAKS TO **FERGUS** VIA THE MICROPHONE LINK WITH THE COMPUTER) Fergus, don't panic. The rocket scientists are just trying to rattle your cage. They want you to think you're being attacked by aliens.

<u>FERGUS:</u> (V.O.)
(SHOUTS) Thanks lads. I'll deal with them.

SCENE 15. INT. ROCKET SCIENCE ROOM. SAME TIME.

PRITH, **NORA** AND **JACK** ARE WATCHING **FERGUS** ON THE MONITORS.

PRITH:
Oh my word. He's threatening the spacecraft with a toilet brush.

NORA:
He's either very brave or very stupid.

JACK:
I know which one I'd pick.

NORA:
You have to admire his gumption though. He's throwing loo rolls at it as well.

PRITH:

What's he's dragging along the ground like a sack of potatoes?

JACK:

It's a sack of potatoes.

PRITH:

He's lobbing them at the spacecraft's lights. Oh great shot. He got them right on their main beacon.

JACK:

They'll zap him any minute now.

PRITH SUDDENLY NOTICES AN ALARM WARNING ON ONE OF THE MONITORS.

PRITH:

Someone's hacking into our computer system.

NORA:
Who is it?

PRITH:
(TAPS QUICKLY AT THE KEYBOARD) Fergus' Pack–a–Pubs. They're situated in the old croft on the other side of the loch.

JACK:
I knew I'd seen weird comings and goings.

PRITH:
There's a message for us from, Alvie. He's sending us a raspberry and telling us to get stuffed. (READS ON) Apparently they think we're trying to frighten them with a fake spacecraft.

JACK:
Stupid was the correct option then.

SCENE 16. INT. WORKROOM. SAME TIME.

ALVIE AND **TEAPOT** ARE CHEERING **FERGUS** ON TO VICTORY.

ALVIE:
Go on yourself, Fergus.

TEAPOT:
(CHEERS) Their mangy spaceship is backing away. We win! We win!

A MESSAGE COMES THROUGH ON THE COMPUTER FOR **ALVIE**.

ALVIE:
Uh–oh.

TEAPOT:
(READS THE MESSAGE) Stuff you too — but it's not us. PS — if you keep our secrets, we'll keep yours. Deal?

ALVIE AND **TEAPOT** NOD IN AGREEMENT.

ALVIE:
(TYPES REPLY) Deal.

ALVIE AND **TEAPOT** WATCH **FERGUS** CONTINUING TO FIGHT THE ALIEN SPACESHIP.

TEAPOT:
Should we tell him?

ALVIE:
Nah, they're heading away, he's chased them off. We'll tell him later.

ALVIE AND **TEAPOT** CHEER AS **FERGUS** WINS THE FIGHT.

SCENE 17. INT. WORKROOM — NEXT DAY [17.00]

FERGUS AND **ALVIE** ARE WORKING. AGAIN, THEY LOOK LIKE THEY'VE BEEN IN A SAWDUST SNOWSTORM. **FERGUS** PUTS THE FINISHING TOUCHES TO AN OLD UKULELE. **ALVIE** IS WRAPPING UP A PUB LANTERN.

FERGUS:
Do you think we can trust the rocket scientists to keep our business quiet?

ALVIE:
I reckon they'll keep their mouths shut for now, but we'll just have to play it by ear.

TEAPOT COMES INTO THE WORKROOM FROM OUTSIDE. HE HAS A BAG FULL OF GROCERIES, AND IS WEARING A FAKE MOUSTACHE AND SUNGLASSES.

TEAPOT:
Let me have a go. (GRABS THE UKULELE AND STRUMS IT) I used to be good on the piano.

FERGUS GRABS IT BACK OFF HIM.

FERGUS:
Did you see the scientists on your way back from the town?

TEAPOT:
I caught a glimpse of Nora. I waved to her, but I don't think she recognised me.

FERGUS AND **ALVIE** EXCHANGE A DOUBTFUL LOOK.

TEAPOT:
I know what you're thinking. She knew fine who I was, but a woman like her wouldn't look twice at the likes of me.

ALVIE:
Not at all. I'm sure she did a double–take, especially with that moustache.

TEAPOT TAKES HIS DISGUISE OFF AND UNPACKS THE GROCERIES AT THE TEA MAKING AREA.

FERGUS:
Probably better to keep our distance. We don't know how far we can trust them.

TEAPOT:
(NODS) True enough. I wouldn't know how to deal with a woman like Nora anyway. I'd always feel I'd have to know what I was talking about.

ALVIE:
I bet they'll think twice before messing with us, especially you, Fergus. I'd love to have seen their faces when they saw you fighting off that spaceship.

__FERGUS:__
(SHUDDERS) I've nightmares just thinking about it.

TEAPOT TAKES A PACKET OF MICROWAVEABLE CHIPS FROM THE GROCERY BAG.

__TEAPOT:__
I got us microwave chips for our tea tonight in case the potatoes were contaminated with outer space radiation. (SMILES) Don't want us glowing in the dark.

FERGUS PEERS THROUGH THE PERISCOPE.

__FERGUS:__
Speaking about things glowing in the dark, I think the scientists are spying on us with infrared security sights. Have a look over there.

ALVIE HAS A LOOK THROUGH THE PERISCOPE.

ALVIE:
They're probably as suspicious of us as we are of them.

FERGUS GOES OVER TO ONE OF THE COMPUTERS AND STARTS TYPING IN INSTRUCTIONS.

FERGUS:
I'm switching on the scrambler to stop them listening in to our conversations.

TEAPOT:
I'll put the kettle on — and the micro chips.

AS **TEAPOT** PINGS OPEN THE MICROWAVE OVEN TO PUT THE CHIPS IN, **FERGUS** SWITCHES ON THE SCRAMBLER.

SCENE 18. INT. ROCKET SCIENCE ROOM. SAME TIME.

PRITH, **NORA** AND **JACK** ARE WATCHING THEIR MONITORS, SPYING ON **FERGUS** AND HIS LADS. **PRITH** IS WEARING A LISTENING DEVICE WITH WIRES ATTACHED.

PRITH:
I heard them say something dubious about micro chips — then the sound cut off. (FLICKS A SWITCH) Not a peep, maybe they're using a surveillance scrambler.

JACK:
(SNEERS) As if. They wouldn't know how to scramble an egg by the looks of them.

NORA:
(SUSPICIOUS) Micro chips? What would flat–pack pub builders want with that type of technology?

__PRITH:__
We'll keep a watchful eye on them from now on . . .

PRITH, **NORA** AND **JACK** NOD IN AGREEMENT.

SCENE 19. INT. WORKROOM. A SHORT TIME LATER.

FERGUS, **ALVIE** AND **TEAPOT** ARE ENJOYING THEIR DINNER, EATING CHIP BUTTIES AND DRINKING CUPS OF TEA. THE THREE OF THEM RAISE THEIR CUPS.

FERGUS, ALVIE and TEAPOT:
Cheers!

END

AREA 52 - Subsequent Episodes

Special Forces

Fergus gets a tip–off that a dodgy business competitor from London and his henchmen are on their way up to Area 52. Confident they can give them the run–around, and a good thrashing if it comes to it, Fergus, Alvie and Teapot don their home knitted black balaclava gear and practice their stealth techniques. As luck would have it, the London gang can't find Area 52 and end up in the Shetlands. Unluckily, a team of Special Forces men are on a survival training weekend in one of the bleakest and most remote areas of Scotland — yes, Area 52. Mistaking them for the London rivals, Fergus and the lads give the Special Forces a run for their money — with the reluctant help of the rocket scientists. For the Pack–a–Pubs lads it really is a case of Who Dares Wins!

Varnishing Fiona

Alvie is distressed when he unwittingly varnishes an old newspaper from a pile they'd brought up with them from London. The paper is several years out of date, and while varnishing it as part of the traditional pub decor he reads that his childhood sweetheart, Fiona, has married his archenemy. Alvie's soul searching about his long lost love and missed romantic opportunities causes Fergus to wonder whether he should take a chance and ask Rainy the remote receptionist for a date. (Rainy is Fergus' remote receptionist who is based somewhere else and is heard throughout the series but never seen). Meanwhile, Teapot has discovered that Fiona has since been divorced. Should he tell Alvie? And should he ask Nora Blonde for a date? Fate and the usual mayhem conspire against them.

DIY — (Destroy–It–Yourself)

Crumble Croft is in need of DIY repair and decoration. (This is where Fergus, Alvie and Teapot live). It is a small cottage–like house next to the main Pack–a–Pubs workshop that used to belong to Fergus' grandmother. Rather than having the typical old–fashioned chintz wallpaper and net curtains, granny was a bit of a hippy in her day, and psychedelic sixties decor was more her style. Fergus decides to use some of this stuff to create a retro–chic theme pub for a nightclub owner. The trouble starts when they discover granny had a secret life hidden underneath the floorboards — a tunnel that leads to the rocket scientists' base – and the scientists have been pilfering from granny's hidden hoard. Fergus wants the items back, but Professor Prith is reluctant, especially as it could destroy the launch of their new rocket.

The Lochless Monster

The rocket scientists repeated diving in Area 52's murky loch results in disturbing a monster from its depths. Poking its head above the water to see who's causing the disruption, it is seen by a wily eyed local who reports the sighting of the elusive monster. With the thought of this becoming headline news and attracting loads of tourists, Fergus and his lads team up with the rocket scientists to thwart the gossip. It's up to Fergus to build a fake monster out of wood, and stick it in the loch to make the locals think it was all a prank. This plans works, but then the real monster objects to its mimic, which causes chaos for Fergus and the scientists.

Glow in the Dark

Fergus agrees to take on an order to build two Irish pubs, a Scottish tavern and a posh English bar for a rich client. The man also wants Fergus to design fashionable outfits for the bar staff and redesign the chef's hat. Stuck for ideas, and working to a tight deadline, Fergus and the lads grudgingly recruit the help of the rocket scientists (in exchange for something the scientists need from them) to create the clothes. Not only do the silver and white outfits glow in the dark, they also inadvertently pick up radio signals within a two–mile radius.

Bop 'Till You Drop

Teapot has a secret passion for Ballroom and Latin dancing. He's got medals for his foxtrot and quickstep. To impress Nora Blonde, he gives her an impromptu display of his fancy footwork at the edge of the loch. When Nora gets a glimpse of his salsa in the moonlight, she looks at him in a whole new light. Not to be outdone, Fergus and Alvie decide to learn some of Teapot's moves during their tea breaks. Who knew the rumba would cause so much trouble.

Paparazzi Trouble

When one of Fergus' themed flat–pack pubs wins a popular bar award, the tabloids come sneaking around Area 52 to find Fergus' secret location after a tip–off from a rival in London. However, the paparazzi underestimate the lengths Fergus and the others will go to protect their secrets when they attempt to take photographs of Fergus and his hideout. This is the paparazzi's first mistake.

Night Of The Creepy Cat

During a dark and stormy night, an electricity cut leaves the rocket scientists without any power. Fergus' paranoia comes in handy because he has a contingency plan for such events and has enough self–generated energy to keep his business ticking over until the power comes back on. The scientists have to give in and ask Fergus to help them power one of their mini–rockets which is scheduled for launching. Fergus agrees, but only if he can press the ignition button. Professor Prith agrees and ends up wishing he hadn't. Meanwhile, Alvie sees a large cat prowling near Area 52 when it's dark. Is it a figment of his imagination, just a shadow in the night, or will it come out and attack them during the rocket launch?

Snow Blonde

Two weeks of snow have transformed Area 52 into a winter wonderland. For a bit of fun, Fergus has made snowboards for them. They've never snowboarded in their lives, but how hard can it be? They're all set when Professor Prith sends them an urgent message — Nora Blonde is missing! She went out to defrost one of the rocket science experiments and hasn't come back. She was wearing a white ski suit, white boots, white everything. How hard will it be to find a blonde in the snow? Meanwhile, the dodgy business competitor from London and his henchmen are still trying to locate Fergus' business. They decide to hire the ultimate human bloodhound, someone guaranteed to find anyone in any location — a London taxi driver. Bob is on his way. Within 24 hours he's nailed them. But can he help them find a blonde in a blizzard?

www.ingramcontent.com/pod-product-compliance
Ingram Content Group UK Ltd.
Pitfield, Milton Keynes, MK11 3LW, UK
UKHW020135250726
13967UKWH00002B/670

9 781908 072375